DAILY UPGRADE

How to Trust God

And

Receive an Upgrade

By

JACK ROTHENFLUE

ISBN-13: 978-1722357160
ISBN-10: 1722357169

TO ORDER BOOK : www.Amazon.com (including Amazon international sites) Search for "Daily Upgrade".

Jesus Laughing Picture.
Copyright 1977 Praise Screen Prints, Jesuslaughing.com. Used with permission.

COVER PHOTO:
Jack's awesome companion and road warrior. Cooper shows us how to REST.

Table of Contents

Introduction

Humbly I come to the point of explanation. As you read, you will be looking into my private life and personal history. In my mind, these devotionals were never intended to be published, much less compiled into a book. So one of my life-scriptures pops up at this point as the Lord once said, "...the way I work surpasses the way you work and the way I think is beyond the way you think..." Isaiah 55:9 (MSG). In other words, it is as if Father is saying, "Get over yourself and let Me lead".

For over 20 years, I have been given prophetic words and comments by many to "write a book". So, why have I waited this long, you might ask? Maybe it was because I didn't think that what I wrote was that profound or I thought ,"Yep that's what the world really needs, another daily devotional". Truthfully, I did not want to do the work. Simply, I was in rebellion and that is not a good place to be before the God of all creativity.

You will be reading my history as it evolves in real time and in it, you might see some shifts in my thinking, as I learned along the way. In 2005, my son Lee approached me saying that he needed something encouraging to get him started early in the day. So I said, "Well maybe I could send you something." And so it began as I added my daughter Sheri, at her request. That was it, just my two wonderful kids. Therefore, in 2005 I sent my first morning email for the workday. It finally ended at the end of 2011 when my ministry was very demanding and I could no longer devote the time needed. Simple right?

Well along the way, others expressed interest so that at one point, I believe I was sending these to about 80 people. Honestly most days, it was a chore because I do not enjoy writing. There, I said it! I will admit however, that once I started putting words on the page, it came easily. Yeah, go figure. Ultimately, it became a joy to send my kids a bit of my heart. Why, you ask?   I intended this to be a way to encourage, inform and train them to develop a faith-life that included, quiet time with the Lord of their life. I believe that because of the chaotic and often toxic world that surrounds us, we need The Truth. I believe that comes during times of intimacy with Father-God, which produces a peace and confidence. Therefore, it is not optional. Faith-life is lifesaving. Intimacy with the One who loves unconditionally is the secret to real peace and joy.

As I said, this was written daily, so I chose to leave the historical comments embedded as history unfolded along the way. It was written as a conversation, so you may sense an informal feel as you read. As I write, I would see Jesus as joyful, smiling and even laughing at times. As I would focus on that image, it would often change my mood. I believe it is the true image of our amazing God Who loves our presence.

I decided to call this faith journey with my adult kids a "Daily Upgrade" using Graham Cooke's often-used term. Why is it an upgrade? It is because life's challenges require a response. I have discovered that it is best to respond after asking the Lord to show us the situation from a higher perspective. And you know what? Our Father in heaven is pleased to give us a divine upgrade. Please enjoy your personal upgrade.....daily.

NOTE: All full capitalizations, underlines, and single quotation marks are my personal emphasis.

The sentence, "It is not essential that we understand everything, but that we trust God in everything" is by Graham Cooke in his book *Hiddenness and Manifestation.*

Thanksgivings

There could be a long list of people that I would like to thank, who were encouragers in helping get this book published. It has been a 20-year journey. Foremost, I am thankful to my Co-Pilot, The Holy Spirit of the Living God. If His love for me resulted in any inspiration you may experience while reading these devotionals, I am most blessed. They are Grace-laced for sure.

Next would be my awesome wife of 50 years. Carol has been the perfect pastors' wife, friend and partner in ministry for over 41 years of serving together. A typical example would be when I told her I was going to find someone to type the manuscript and as usual, she volunteered without being asked. Thanks Babe!

Graham Cooke, prophet, speaker, author and founder of Brilliant Book House.com is a key player for me. He has sowed into my life for over 21 years. Graham has been my long-distance teacher through his books, teachings and even a personal encounter a few times when he prayed for me. He has changed my perspective of encountering our God of Grace who Graham calls the "the kindest person I've ever met". **I give the following disclaimer**: "Many of my writings have been inspired by Graham Cooke's heart. Because I wrote these originally as a personal private devotion to my kids, I never made note when I was directly quoting him verbatim. So, my paraphrases are in the book, as well. I have tried to quote him where I knew it was verbatim because I want to honor this amazing man of God's own heart.

Finally, my thanks to many encouragers such as one of our faithful intercessors Barbara, as well as Rick, Chris, Sylvia and others who have also published. I remain humbled by the many folks who have said to me, "You need to write a book". Well, now I have, so, thanks.

DAY 1

THE FAITH JOURNEY

So what is life's journey about? A non-believer might say many things, but the truth is that it is the same for all peoples. The journey we call "life" is about finding and knowing God. That is why you may hear that the journey is more important than any one moment. Some others say that the journey is more important than the destination (because while on planet Earth, all we have is the journey).

Ok... if the journey is finding God, why does it seem so difficult at times? Graham Cooke, my master-teacher, says that God plays hide and seek. Sometimes we can feel or hear His presence and most of the time, it seems, we "feel or hear" nothing. The Bible says "seek and you shall find, knock and the door will be opened", (Matthew 7:7-8). I believe every persistent one will get what he asks for. Everyone who knocks persistently will, one day, find an open door. "One day" simply encourages us to never give up. Never!

Well, with God it is always about romance. He must always lead the dance. He is luring you to His heart but it takes faith to find Him. The Bible says that the only way you can please God is to have faith. Faith is being sure and certain of what you cannot put your finger on ('paraphrase' Hebrew 11:1). The Lord is constantly teaching us how to expand and deepen our faith so we can KNOW Him better.

In fact, He may starve your soul (mind, body, emotions) to feed your spirit. Jesus was baptized and the Heavenly Father spoke to the crowd a wonderfully good Word about Him and the next thing you know He is in the wilderness without any food. A moment full of promise and then an isolated emptiness. Why? Because God wants us to be in a place where it is Him or nothing. Like the Israelites wandering in the wilderness without any stores or shops for 40 years. The people of Israel in the desert and free from bondage but no food. Here comes God each morning with food for the day and shoes that would not wear out for the entire journey. The Israelites were on a sacred journey, but often a mysterious one.

God is training us to know that He is our food, our provision, as we seek Him first (Matthew 6:33). So, if you speak to the Lord and get no feeling or word, He IS speaking, but straight to your spirit, bypassing your mind and building your faith for future use.

Graham Cooke says there are "no good days or bad days in the Kingdom, just days of grace. Some days God gives us grace to enjoy the day and other times, enough grace to endure the day." Enjoy this day of grace, compliments of your Faithful God. Let us go on a journey together and receive a daily upgrade of our relationship with Jesus.

"It is not essential that we understand everything,
but that we trust God in everything."

DAY 2

PERSEVERANCE IS THE KEY

The Love of God. Wow!!! How can we understand it? Answer? We never will totally, and that's the good news. It is so beyond our finite mind's comprehension, that His love will always be big enough (Ephesians 3:14-21).

Can God's real love get through to us? Sometimes we close ourselves off from the goodness of God because we are so depressed about our own performance, or lack thereof, as a Christian. But that is so negative and God is so positive. Why spend our day thinking about what we are NOT?

You see, God loves us for who we are RIGHT NOW...the good, the bad and even the ugly. Hard to believe? Yes, and you know why? Because we may be comparing God's way of love to those we know on earth and trying to somehow magnify it to be bigger. The problem is that we will never make it big enough. He loves us for who we are going to be as well. And yes, He knows exactly what that will look like. I love a verse in a praise song called "I knew What I Was Getting Into", speaks God's heart saying, "I knew what I was getting into when I called you. I knew what I was getting into but I love you just the same."

At times in our life, we need to release our will and say, "I'm not going to think that way." And then upgrade our image of God. We can cooperate with establishing a new image in our hearts as negative forces come our way. The fruit of the Spirit (Galatians 5:22) is grown best in bad soil. If you need to grow in grace, the Lord will send someone who is very difficult for you to be around as a "grace-grower". If you need to learn patience, God will allow something in your life to pop up that will require you to make a choice...<u>stomp around or laugh.</u> You can even ask the Lord to give you scripture that reflects His nature.

Now, don't quit if the first time you try it, you get nothing. Perseverance is the key, at this point and always. Question to self: "Do I want to know Him so deeply that I will say aloud, 'Jesus, I will never give up'".

I believe that God is eager to show us who He is each time we seek Him. Think about the following character traits of our God and creator, complements of Graham Cooke from a CD teaching:

> 'He has immense, immeasurable compassion greater than my sin.
>
> He is shamelessly forgiving, every time. Yes even the 202nd time you ask Him about the same sin.
>
> His grace is a power that enables us to feel good about ourselves.
>
> He is the kindest, happiest, and most joyful person in the universe.
>
> He loves being trusted.
>
> He won't keep a record of our wrongs
>
> He gives us value by giving us Himself (His Holy Spirit).'

Ask, what do I need to change to be able to appropriate the positive attitude of being loved by God? How can my upgrade of the reality of His love splash onto those around me, particularly at home?

"It is not essential that we understand everything, but that we trust God in everything".

DAY 3

HOW TO RECEIVE GOD'S FAVOR

Key: If God has called and equipped us, then He will lead us. He has equipped us to be ruled by the spirit. But it does take an action of our will, which is our part, so that God can do the leading. God has chosen not to rule our will, most of the time.

So why is it such a struggle? Why is it difficult to rule life by the spirit in us? Read Romans 7:14-25 to hear Paul, the apostle's struggle.

As human beings, we are at war with ourselves. Our soul (mind, will and emotions) and our spirit are at odds. If we have accepted Jesus as Lord, then His Spirit and ours are one. This is a supernatural act. Our soul and our spirit compete with one another for control. Each desperately wants to run the show, but only one can at any one moment, but you get to choose. When the Holy Spirit entered us and we became born again, our soul should have bowed the knee to the reign of God. But, the soul can be influenced by the devil, our #1 enemy, and that's why we are told to guard our mind, and our heart (which biblically refers to our soul).

The Spirit hears the whisper of God but we must use our will and tell our mind to get in line under the control of the Spirit. Weird as it sounds, it works. We can say, "I'm not going to think that, so 'mind', bend the knee to my spirit and do what you are told." Our soul refuses to surrender easily because it wants to be number one (so the enemy can gain influence over your life's choices). Example: the soul believes in self-gratification but the Spirit believes that satisfaction comes first from the Lord. Our soul wants to tell us how we are wrong; our spirit wants to tell us who we are in Christ. The soul hates being weak and finds ways to point us to stuff to give us pleasure or power; encourages us to put someone down; flex our muscles through manipulation or confrontation.

We must break our soul power or we will struggle to serve the Lord effectively. If the soul rules, we are left vulnerable to external pressures. Living in the Spirit is THE answer. Once we learn this, nothing from the outside world will be able to shake us.

I want you to live in a FOG (Favor of God). How? You must increase your intimacy with the Lord. (Proverbs 8:34-35 and Psalms 46:10-11).

KEY: Favor comes when we know who God is and who we are in Him. He accomplishes the impossible and creates the incredible. Favor is related to our level of intimacy with God. Now don't make a religious thing of this. Don't make some legal rule or measuring stick. It's simple. The more we know God, the more we hear His heart. The same is true with any close friend, right? We must begin to rest in Him, abide in Him, make our home in Him, and learn to stop long enough to listen. Easy? Nope. Worth it? Yep. Will it happen? Up to ya.

Look, we can either keep on doing what we've been doing and God will help us clean up our messes, OR we can listen to Him first, and make the right choice at the beginning, having fewer messes. At that point, all the Lord has to do is rejoice with us.

In my early ministry, I would tell myself, "Hey, that's a good idea, so let's go for it" and then I'd ask the Lord to follow me as I presented it to the church. Later in life, I learned the difference between a good thing and a God-authored thing. The cool thing about Jesus is that He would follow me into that "good thing" and bless it. What I'm saying is, learn from me and don't repeat this exasperating lifestyle. Let God lead. Stop and ask, "Lord, how do you want to lead this dance?" Seek first the King.

"It is not essential that we understand everything,
but that we trust God in everything".

DAY 4

PICTURE OF GOD

The Lord's favor is available to each of us. Graham Cooke says, "As we upgrade our image of who God is for us, we increase our favor". In fact, the antidote to stress and crisis is upgrading our fellowship with God. Moses understood when he said in Exodus 33:15-16, "If Your presence does not go with us, do not bring us up from here. How then will it be known that your people and I, have found grace in Your sight."

The Holy Spirit is working to establish us in Christ. Our goal then, is to cooperate with the Holy Spirit and stay focused on Him in the process. God knows who He is and He loves what He does. He wants you to know the same. The more you have a wrong picture of God, the more religious and legalistic you get. We aren't in a religion, we are in a Person. The Spirit of Jesus lives in us as believers.

Who is God? He is a gentle Father, always gracious, always good, always confident and peaceful. He is generous, consistent, unchangeable, everlasting and faithful. What is your vision of God? Your image dictates your view of life and therefore, your view of those around you. Your perception drives your perspective; your perspective influences how you engage others.

Seeing Him as your Prince of Peace, your provider, means you aren't allowed to worry any more. Graham Cooke says, "You simply cannot trust God and worry at the same time, one has to go and you get to choose." Every time we are in need, it should be an adventure because we are not intimidated. We should be fascinated about what God will do, asking, "I wonder how He will do this one?" Conflict will eventually be an opportunity to see His provision through us as we step back into Him and ask for His perspective. The soul reacts and the

Spirit responds. One is spontaneous and the other reflective. One is driven through natural instinct and the other by spiritual excellence.

Examples:

His promise: Hebrew 13:5 — *"Don't love money; be satisfied with what you have. For God has said, "I will never fail you. I will never abandon you".*

His joy: Psalms 25:6 — *"Remember, O Lord, your compassion and unfailing love, which you have shown from long ages past".*

His consistency: Psalms 121:4 — *"Indeed, he who watches over Israel never slumbers or sleeps".*

His Name: Revelation 19:11 — *"Then I saw heaven opened, and a white horse was standing there. Its rider was named Faithful and True, for he judges fairly and wages a righteous war".*

Write down your picture of God. Is it time for an upgrade? What is your image of your Creator/Deliverer? Is your image consistent with the biblical images? What do you need to change?

"It is not essential that we understand everything,
but that we trust God in everything".

DAY 5

KEY TO INTIMACY

What we have been talking about are foundational issues of being in relationship with the Lord. We must do the first commandment (Exodus 20:1-2) and the great commandment (John 13:34). Everything is wrapped up in those two. Our lives must be led by our spirit and Matthew 6:33 is how that happens. Again, when I say, "our spirit", I am referring to our one-in-Christ Spirit. We are talking about things that are of 'prime' importance.

Let's look at a story in which Jesus illustrates the point. Read Luke 10:38-42.

Here's a contrast in someone living through their souls and another living through their spirit. Martha was not doing anything bad. She was preparing to feed her special guest and friend. But Jesus said, "you are worried about many things…but only one thing is needed." Did ya get that? Jesus narrowed our following Him to one thing. Pretty simple, huh?

Referring to Mary, He said, "(she) has chosen that good part, which will not be taken away from her." In the NLT version it reads, "Mary has discovered it and I won't take it away from her." What was that? Her spirit was drawn and energized by the person Jesus; therefore, she sat at His feet, undistracted, and listened. He spoke, she soaked. The one thing? Jesus.

The issue here is what is primary or of first order? Martha's concerns were legitimate but she moved into her soul (emotion) and spoke against her sister in an emotional outburst. This is what happens when we are NOT living from the inside out. This story suggests that we must place value on His presence. Although we can't sit at His feet

24/7, the story illustrates what can happen when we go first to our spirit to direct our path. Here was Jesus teaching a significant life truth. How do I know? He said it was the "one thing" to develop intimacy with Him. Martha was in another place physically and spiritually. Seemed right? But was it right at that moment? Maybe it was her "place' in the kitchen. Nevertheless, Jesus was profoundly making a key point to living in the spirit.

Does the presence of God have primacy in our lives? Or does, work, play, TV, couch sitting? None of these are sinful; it is just a matter of priorities. What are we normally thinking about? Worldly, temporal stuff or eternal stuff? I suggest that if we learn to rest in the Lord, we will still accomplish the "other" stuff but in proper order. Like John Wimber said, explaining how to release the Christ in us, "Just do the stuff".

Now, y'all, this is not a guilt-trip version of the Daily Upgrade. We all need to re-think where we are with Him. But when we live in our spirit, we will not need reassurance. We will have a built-in testimony that we are sons and daughters of the most high God. Let's fight against giving power to the temporal "stuff' and just lean back and rest in the Lord's presence for a moment (whatever that might be for you).

The challenge: let's find some time today where we take a moment for God...a moment WHOLLY devoted to resting in His presence. Focusing on Him. Remember, He said, "I will never leave you or forsake you". He is always present and therefore, available.

"It is not essential that we understand everything,
but that we trust God in everything".

DAY 6

SPIRIT INSTRUCTED LIFE

Ok, so how did the challenge go? Find any extra time? Now if your answer is "nope", just remember that you <u>will</u> eventually win. If not today, then tomorrow, because you are a son and daughter of the most high God. Never give up.

We were created with three components. We are body, soul (mind, will, emotions) and spirit. The number "3" is biblically significant as it symbolizes a divine matter, or a Godly moment. Examples are when Jesus said, "three days and I will rise again"; The Trinity=Father, Son, Holy Spirit; God's description of Jonah inside the belly of the fish for three days; and John saying, "we have these three witnesses, the Spirit, the water and the blood, and the three agree". (John 5:7)

The scriptural reference that nails our specific issue today is I Thessalonians 5:23 "Now, may the God of peace and harmony set you apart, making you completely holy. And may your entire being, 'spirit, soul, and body' be kept completely flawless in the appearing of our Lord Jesus, the anointed one". (Passion translation). There you have it. We are made up of three distinct parts all of which makes us whole while on earth.

Life shows us that body and soul often work together against the spirit. We seem to go the soul or body first, ie: "oh my head aches", or "I look terrible so they won't like me"; "I'm not important"; "I'll never get this". But if we were following the design of God, it would be (Matthew 6:33) "I'll think God first. I'll see what the Lord shows me about this". In God's design, He intended His spirit to dwell mingled with our spirit and for His spirit to rule our lifestyle. We are not human beings having a temporary spiritual experience rather we are spiritual beings having a temporary human experience while on earth.

To have the fullest expression of Christ, our soul must understand it cannot act on its own. Our spirit gives our soul instruction. Sounds weird, I know, but we should consider what God's original intention was and try to get back on board with Him, and align with His design. Our soul needs to be saved (redeemed) everyday.

Look at the scriptures that support the spirit life: Romans 7:22, Ephesians 3:16-17, Romans 8:8, II Corinthians 4:16, to name a few.

The truth is that God does NOT live in our soul or body. We were made in His image and we are told that He is Spirit (John 4:24). So, the only place He can dwell is in our spirit. That also means that the only place from which His wisdom and power comes to us through the spirit. Simply put, we aren't great enough to get it 'right' by our intellect, emotional stability, strong willpower, or strong backs. When we check in with the Spirit, then we allow Him to get it 'right' in us. Like the story I once heard about the grandmother who saw a car trap a small child under its weight. She screamed "Lord help me" and His spirit told her mind to go to the car, told her emotions to stay calm, and told her muscles to lift the car up and pull the child out. She and God saved that child.

God is so cool. He knew that our body and soul would eventually wear out. But our spirit is eternal. God always works in that which will last. He is not focused on what we look like or what we do, but He is concerned about who we are. He always sees our true motives.

Challenge: Let's try to talk to ourselves in the midst of "our stuff" and tell our soul or body to get in line behind and under the control of our spirit. Let's see what happens. If at first we don't succeed...well, you know the rest.

"It is not essential that we understand everything, but that we trust God in everything".

DAY 7

RELEASING THE HOLY SPIRIT

We have been talking about the 'spirit', so let's dig deeper. Who or what is the 'Spirit'?

The Spirit is first of all a person, referred to as "He" (Romans 8:26-27). Paul calls Him the "Spirit of Jesus" (I Peter 1:10-11). He (The Spirit) is that part of us that finds refuge in God (Psalms 91). He is a place inside of us that cannot be touched by anything in the world because The Spirit lives as the presence of God in our spirit. Yet to interact with the physical world, the 'Spirit' must operate through our body and soul. Therein lies the rub; the mystery.

What does the Spirit look like? The Bible says He is our refuge, strong high tower, and hiding place where we can hide in the shadow of His wings (Psalms 91). So one of our tasks, as we develop spiritually, is to learn how to access the place of the 'Spirit'. The process? First <u>pause and fix your eyes on Jesus</u> (get a personal image). Intellectually, <u>tell yourself to move into the place of your spirit and then rest and relax to receive His wisdom and peace</u>. At first, we will have to exercise our will, 1 but eventually it will be "normal" for us to move supernaturally. Nope, we may not be there yet. We're a work in progress. Most of our difficulty is not with others, but with ourselves. Am I just talking to myself here?

Simply, yet profoundly, we must allow (an act of the will) our life to be governed by our 'spirit'. Our spirit is to control the way we act and speak and lead. And the cool news is that God's power then becomes available to us so that it can actually happen. How do I know? Experience, yes, but there's more. You see, for the born again believer, our 'spirit' is supernaturally co-mingled with His Holy Spirit (Acts 2:38). So once we tap into our spirit, we simultaneously tap into His Holy Spirit. (Re-read this paragraph slowly). In fact, you may want to print it out and study it today from time to time. This is the key to how we live in the power of God as Paul teaches. *"However, you are not in the flesh but in the Spirit, if indeed the Spirit of God dwells in you. But if anyone does not have the Spirit of Christ, he does not belong to Him". (Romans 8:9)*

Personal confession: I lived as a Christian until, at 32 years old, I first learned that the 'Spirit', was a person of the Trinity and not an "it". I lived saved and heaven-bound but without the knowledge or power of His 'Spirit' to guide me. Oh, He guided me anyway because of His incredible Love and MERCY. I was not aware that the infilling of the Holy Spirit was a real deal. Simply, I discovered that once I personally accepted (asked for) His infilling, then a new power and dimension of His presence became available. Please take a moment and read Matthew 3:11, John 1:33, Acts 1:15-16, 9:17-18, 10:44-48, and 19:1-6. Our desire moves us toward God and He completes the transaction. Simply, it is a release of His 'Spirit' in you as you ask for Him to fill you with Himself.

Ok, that's enough for now. Plenty right? But my precious friends, this is the foundation of a brand new way to live. I have found that there is no better way to walk with God than through His 'Spirit'. After all, He makes it available and so why not take everything He has for us.

"It is not essential that we understand everything,
but that we trust God in everything".

DAY 8

HOW TO RULE YOUR SOUL

Our soul is not our enemy, because God created it in us. Yet, our soul wants to meet God on its terms. The soul wants God to do things for it while running its own life. It treats God like an insurance policy, when something is beyond our capability, and we cry out for the Spirit of God. But the soul was designed to serve the God of all creation.

How do you know your soul is ruling? It will create religious stuff like rules, controls and things you must accomplish in order to maintain your destiny. It is more concerned with retaining its power than being a servant; aware of status rather than humility (Philippians 2:1-11); tries to lead with power rather than being led with wisdom. The natural soul is clever not wise. The soul will always draw you into contrast and comparison; how you view yourself against others.

This may sound weird, but it makes sense if you consider what makes up your soul. As I said, It is your mind, will and emotions. Are you getting this?

Before we came to the Lord, our spirit lay asleep in us with no concept of God. We lived as we pleased. No one was allowed to mentor us as we made up our minds for our own benefit and pleasure. A good example is a 2 yr. old. But when God breaks in, fills us with his Spirit, the battle begins within. Now our soul has competition and is no longer in full control. It is a daily battle for supremacy, a conflict of two natures (Romans 7:14-15).

Today, let's just meditate on which part of us is in control at this moment. Take note of how you think, behave or speak. Just be aware about being judgmental. This is just an experiment in introspection (looking within with an analytical eye). Then, reflect to see how you can move toward your spirit taking control. An example of this in my own life is during a season where a man in one of the churches I served was trying to get me fired. He was very clever and my natural soul took control. My body would tighten and my emotions would go dark every time I was in his presence. Then one day (after years of soulish behavior and thinking), I forgave him. I joined my one-in-Christ Spirit and it changed my perspective. Never again did I feel negative when I was with him.

Now if any of this is confusing, remember God is not the author of confusion. Just relax and keep moving toward Him. In fact, why not just ask Him to show you the next right move today.

"It is not essential that we understand everything,
but that we trust God in everything".

DAY 9

WHY CAN THE SOUL DOMINATE?

How did your introspection go? Did you notice when your thinking comes from soul versus your spirit? Your soul concentrates on pleasing you. Your spirit is all about pleasing God and others.

Now y'all, we are going to be in Romans for a few days.

Romans 5:1 *"We have been made right in God's sight by (our) faith"*. Notice it is NOT by our effort or intellectual understanding. The result? "We have peace with God BECAUSE of what Jesus Christ HAS DONE for us. Notice it is past tense; it's a done deal. Being right with God is not based on how well we do, act or think. This is a <u>key</u> truth from scripture. Being right with God is based on what Jesus did for us on the cross.

Bottom Line: Pressure is off!!

Romans 5:3 suggests problems and trials are good for us. Why? Problems help us learn endurance... Yes, we are called disciples, meaning learners. God favors endurance. He loves it when we hang in there no matter what, hanging on His promises. Why is endurance good for us? Romans 5:4, *"endurance develops strength of character and character strengthens our confident hope..."* As we hang in there, God is building our 'character' and at the same time our 'confidence'. I believe that the peace of God is actually a "confidence" in who He is and what He can do. Then Paul says in vs. 5... *"This hope will NOT lead to disappointment."*

Let's get the above down in our spirit, not just our mind, will and emotions. Romans 6: 13 encourages us to *"give yourselves completely to God..."* Why? *"...you have new life."* Romans 6:14, *"Sin is no longer your master. You live under freedom of God's grace"*. Meaning? (Vs 16), *"...you can choose to be a slave to sin, which leads to death, or you can choose to obey God, which leads to righteous living".* You are 'FREE' to choose each and every time you are confronted by darkness. One has to go. You get to choose because God created you with a will to choose.

Romans 6: 22 says that …you are free from the 'POWER' of sin. Meaning? Sin will continue to come knocking because your #1 enemy hates you and wants to ruin your life on earth. Your soul is where he thinks he can have dominion. But you are free from its power to overwhelm you because you have power in the Spirit to overcome the enemy's pull. Move into your spirit and your #1 enemy has to quit. Try it, because it really works. Tell your #1 enemy (aloud) "Shut up. You either go back to hell or to the feet of Jesus for permission to mess with me. Go NOW!" You may want to re-read this a time or two. But I think it's a powerful foundation for a new way to live; a new lifestyle based upon the lifestyle demonstrated by Jesus.

"It is not essential that we understand everything,
but that we trust God in everything".

THE DAILY BATTLE

A little more from Romans

Romans 7 tells us about our power and our powerlessness. When we are born again, religious rules no longer hold you in its power. In verse: 4 Paul suggests that sin will not conquer you, for God already has taken care of that. You are not governed by law but governed by the reign of the grace of God. What's the bottom line here? We do not follow a religion; we follow a Person in the name of Jesus. It's not about rules, it's about relationship. That truth should be comforting.

In the old days, when we were controlled by our sinful desires (selfishness), we often felt guilty but went ahead anyway feeling, sometimes, as if we were powerless to do anything. Paul, in Romans 7:6, tells us that we have been fully released from the power of the law (religious thinking) because we are no longer a prisoner to the power of selfishness. Yes, we are still selfish at times, but we always have a powerful way out and it's called 'life in the Spirit'. We still have sinful urges, but sin is NOT the inner-motor that rules our lives. Now we have the privilege of choosing to live our lives influenced by the Spirit.

The purpose of the "law" (Old Testament) was to show what sin looks like. Verse 7 reminds us that we can see how terrible sin really is because we have something righteous to compare sin to. You see, if a mother tells a child to "Go steal some food because we are poor and that is the way we survive", she becomes the standard. The Bible shows us what is right and wrong and becomes a permanent standard that is not based upon what we feel at the moment. Our decisions are not based on what we need, rather, they are based upon God's heart.

Without a solid moral standard, we become the one who chooses, at the moment, what seems right.

Now read versus 15-21. (I'll wait). '*I don't really understand myself, for I want to do what is right, but I don't do it. Instead, I do what I hate. But if I know that what I am doing is wrong, this shows that I agree that the law is good. So, I am not the one doing wrong; it is sin living in me that does it. And I know that nothing good lives in me, that is, in my sinful nature. I want to do what is right, but I can't. I want to do what is good but I don't. I don't want to do what is wrong, but I do it anyway. But if I do what I don't want to do, I am not really the one doing wrong; it is sin living in me that does it. I have discovered this principle of life, that when I want to do what is right, I inevitably do what is wrong*".

Sounds like you could have written it? That's the way I feel too. Life on earth is a struggle of good against bad. It is a war with our mind. That's why Paul teaches us to guard our mind and what goes into it by our hearing or seeing. Porn in, porn out; cussing in cussing out; selfish ideas in, selfish behavior out. It is a war and some days I wonder who won.

But...Who will free me from this war? Romans 7:24-25 (NLT) says, "*Oh, what a miserable person I am! Who will free me from this life that is dominated by sin and death? Thank God*!". The answer is in Jesus Christ our Lord. So you see how it is that in my mind I really want to obey God's law, but because of my sinful nature I am a slave to sin. Notice the preposition "in" here. That little word is BIG because it reminds us that we must live "in" the spirit of Christ in order to have the power of Christ available to us. It's all about abiding as John teaches us in John 15:1-10. But also, the word "in" reminds us that His Holy Spirit is already 'in' residence 'in' our own spirit. We have what we need forever sealed in our inner person.

That's enough for now. Chew, swallow and digest this food for your spirit.

"It is not essential that we understand everything,
but that we trust God in everything".

FREEDOM RELEASING TRUTH

Finally, we get to chapter 8 of Romans. (open your bible now). It is one of the best teachings on 'life in the Spirit' that our Lord deposited in the hearts of those who wrote the Bible. The verses are coming from the New Living Translation.

Romans 8 is a key scripture to know because of its valuable and practical truth. Verse 1 says, *"There is NO condemnation for those who belong to Christ Jesus."* Whenever your mind begins to tell you something that sounds condemning, it is NOT from the Lord. Period!!!

Romans 8:5 means that "if" we choose to "think" God, then we will be controlled by the Holy Spirit. Those who want to be controlled by God, think about things that come from and please the Spirit of God. Paul calls some of those 'things', *"...honorable, right, pure, lovely and admirable."* (Philippians 4:8).

Romans 8: 9 says that you are controlled by the Spirit IF you have the Spirit of God living in you. Meaning. You 'can' be controlled by the Spirit because you have the right "connection".

Romans 8:12 "Sinful urges " simply means that we can control our urges by our willful choice, moment by moment, test by test, temptation by temptation, because of the power of Jesus in us.

Is this good or what?

Romans 8:23 is simply about our human condition as we "groan" to be released from the pain of living here. Sometimes it ain't fun, right?

Then we see the freedom-producing truth of Romans 8:26. It tells us that the Lord has provided a unique prayer language that sounds like "groanings" but speaks directly to God, bypassing our mind (which can easily muddy up our prayer thoughts). *"He helps us in our weakness"*, Paul says. Romans 8:28 (my wife's favorite) is a promise from God to us. He is always working in our lives and through our experiences for (His) good. He is simply asking us to cooperate. Let's give it a try.

Romans 8:30 and 33 tell us about our *"right standing"* as His kid. We are always on the right side, the side of victory...even when it doesn't feel like it. Feelings are not always faith, ya know.

Romans 8:34 reminds us that Jesus is our #1 intercessor. Condemnation never comes from Him. So folks I say again, if you hear condemning words in your mind, they are n<u>ot</u> from God. This is an important truth. Too many of us walk around with poor self-esteem. But the truth is, we are kids of The one and only unconditional- loving King.

Romans 8:35 explains feelings vs. faith. Please pause and read this verse now. (I'll wait). No matter what we are feeling, His promises STAND, even if our feelings don't validate it. His promises trump our premises.

Romans 8:38-39 are reminders of His power and His steadfastness. Absolutely NOTHING can keep us from His love and His purpose. Nothing. You got it? Nothing!

This may take re-reading because it is power-packed. Take a bite and taste the goodness of the Lord. (Psalms 34:8).

"It is not essential that we understand everything,
but that we trust God in everything".

DAY 12

PRACTICING REST

By now, you are practicing each day to live in and through your spirit, right? It's not about getting it right or being successful. Rather, it's about being a disciple (learner) and practicing (attempting) the discipline and never giving up!

You are thanking, worshipping, and embracing His peaceful confidence in Who He is. You are trying to find a moment to be still, quiet your mind and connect with the Almighty. Stillness promotes a God consciousness. It's a real key, y'all. Just keep 'trying' each day. Our #1 enemy wants you to give up. So whom will you listen to and obey today? Which supernatural power will win? Whose team will you join?

Begin to ask questions. What do you want to teach me in this season, Papa? What can I see in my current situation that I might identify as the Lord's hand? Lord, what must I travel through to get to the next journey? What will be my test? You might write them down so you can see them before you. Graham Cooke says to ask, "Father, who do I need You to be for me in this situation?" Knowing where I'm headed, Lord, what are you about to reveal about Yourself?

Patience is a tool of God to teach trust and to gauge where you are in trusting. Ultimately, when we learn how to rest in Him, no matter what, patience will no longer be needed. Remember that you MUST begin to believe resting is possible so that you can eventually attain that level of confidence. Say it aloud, "I WILL NEVER GIVE UP".

Ask Father to be real to you and ask Him that He deliver all that heaven holds for you. It is not selfish if you are simply asking for what is already prepared for you. If you get any responses to any questions, please write them down and keep them in a handy accessible place.

Why? So you can be reminded of God's faithfulness and be encouraged by your history with God as you re-read them.

KEY: Finally, just "be". For me, John 15 is the key chapter in the New Testament. Jesus speaks here and says ten times in ten verses for the believer to "abide". Other translations use other words to describe the Greek such as, "stay", "make your home", and "remain". Bottom line is that this is another key to deepening the relationship with Him. He wants to hang out with you (Psalm145:18; and Lamentations 3: 57).

Just be still, resting in Him. Don't panic; don't rush out; don't make quick decisions; don't quickly ask another's opinion. Rather just BE with God in the Spirit for a while. Rest: **Relaxed Engaged Simple Trusting.**

Romans 13:14 says, (my paraphrase) "let the Lord Jesus Christ take control of you, and don't think of ways to indulge your evil (natural or soul-based) desires". Simply put, "Let Jesus rule". The word "let" means we have to will it so. It's just a decision moment by moment. We don't have to "DO" it, just ask the Holy Spirit to do it. Then step back in the spirit, rest and watch your loving and capable Father care for you.

"It is not essential that we understand everything,
but that we trust God in everything".

DAY 13

WHOSE ADVICE WILL YOU FOLLOW?

Today we are going to take a deeper look at the inner battle...soul vs spirit. Why? It is of ultimate importance to know whom you battle. It's always best to know your opponent.

It all began with Adam and Eve. They had an envious life of no illness, no stress, no worry, AND they knew God intimately. They walked and talked with Him daily in the garden. Their biggest task? Naming the animals. How hard can that be?

Then came the unspoken question: "whose advice will you follow"? There was the tree of knowledge of good and evil, right there in front of them. Now, if you read Genesis 2 carefully, you will see that they were not longing to eat of this tree until Satan whispered in their ear (to their soul) Genesis Chapter 3:1-5, Satan said, *"Did God, really say you must not eat any of the fruit from any of the trees in the garden?"* Eve says, (my paraphrase) "Well, not the one in the center. If we eat the fruit of that one we'll die". Satan responds, (my paraphrase) "You won't die. God knows that if you will eat the fruit, then you will know all and be like God Himself".

What's interesting here is that there was no evil to worry about at that moment. Deception is the devil's #1 tool. This temptation centered on the issue of wisdom and asks, "Whose advice will you follow?" Of course, in Genesis 2:17 God had said not to eat that fruit, but all the rest of the trees were fine. If we reach across boundaries set by God, we are on a slippery slope.

Here's the deal. Life based on our knowledge alone, is a life without dependence on God. It's like we are saying, "I'll depend on myself, thank you very much". How's that been working for you? In fact, in the book of Judges, we hear the awful accusation by God to Israel as

He sums up the book. *"...All the people did whatever seemed right in their own eyes."* (Judges 21:25) Trying to gain wisdom through knowledge is shallow at best. The wisdom we need for living is found in the tree of life, which is symbolic for God.

Look how silly we are.

What is philosophy? Simply put, it is man's wisdom; how someone thinks about something. Whoop-de-do. The more we babble on about what we think with no God-basis, the more self-absorbed we get. 'Self-absorbed' is another word for 'selfishness' which is another word for sin. Intellect, for some, is their god. In fact, the Bible warned Israel about a pending judgement because they were calling what is "bad", "good" and what is "good", "bad". (Isaiah 5:20:22). Are we there in our day?

Read James 3:15-18. (I'll wait). This is one of the most encouraging scriptures in the New Testament. God's wisdom always lifts us, touches our heart and gives us inspiration and courage. It tells us who we are In-Christ and reminds us of our God-given authority. Verses 17-18 describe "peacemakers" as ones who are the humble, love-driven "kids of the King". It is food for the spirit. You might consider reading this scripture every day for a season.

Adam and Eve and all who have followed them have had to fill the void of power and authority in their lives. We choose either soulish stuff which puffs up OR spiritual stuff which builds up. All peoples have a void in their heart which causes them to be wanted, and there are many things that one can use to attempt to fill it. But, the only lasting source is the Holy Spirit of Jesus. He is here to stay and is our Counselor who brings us wisdom. Try Him. You'll like Him.

"It is not essential that we understand everything,
but that we trust God in everything".

DAY 14

THE DAILY WINABLE WAR

Let's talk once again about our soul. In Mark 4 we find that Jesus was asleep in the boat and a huge storm came up, frightening the disciples. How could He sleep? It was because He had peace and confidence in the Father. They woke Him up, He spoke to the storm and it was immediately over. Fear was conquered by confident peace in His authority. They accused Jesus of not caring, and even today one who lives by the Spirit, may be called "uncaring" if they remain peaceful in a crisis. Actually, it is a confidence that does not require panic.

Anxiety follows the one who lives through the soul but the spiritual one lives in the presence of God. It is a continual battle between the soul and the spirit. Our lives teach us that anxiety never accomplished anything worthwhile.

In the scriptures, while life goes on, we see how our soul can touch the spirit world. That's why the bible teaches us to stay away from mediums, fortune tellers, etc. because we are vulnerable to being influenced. Life in the soul realm offers conditional relationships. What's in it for me? What can I get out of this, etc. Often times, life is about gaining power over another, which is called "a religious spirit" (check out the Pharisees). In this soul life, everything is about feelings. Either my feelings or what I think others are thinking or might think. Feelings are easily wounded if unprotected by the Lord's Spirit. Let the word of God form your self-image.

Some are dominated by their body (how I look) and others by their material possessions. It seems that in this lifestyle, they are consumed about themselves. However, our body and soul were not created to rule our lives because they are incapable of providing a healthy lifestyle.

When Paul wrote his first letter to the Corinthian church, it was all about their soulish approach to living (I Corinthians 5:1-5 & 11:16-22). The church was a mess, as many churches are today.

My point is to remind us that we are in a daily war internally. Soul vs. Spirit. Who will rule our lifestyle? It is a battle and that's why it is so difficult. But it is winnable. Jesus said in John 16, *"There is much more I want to tell you, but you can't bear it now"*, (*Verse 12*) *"All that belongs to the Father is Mine; this is why I said, 'The Spirit will tell you whatever He receives from Me'. (verse 15) "I have told you all this so that you may have peace in me. Here on earth you will have many trials and sorrows. But take heart, because I have overcome the world".(verse 33)*

Your authority: Galatians 5:1 & 5-6 & 13. Please read now.

"It is not essential that we understand everything,
but that we trust God in everything".

DAY 15

MOVING IN THE OPPOSITE SPIRIT

The Lord teaches His kids to be the few on earth who choose to move in the opposite spirit when "dark stuff" comes our way. Hate coming at us, love going back. Pride coming out, humility going back. Betrayal exposed, forgiveness going back. Kind of like our divine mentor, Jesus, who, in a physical and emotional state of carnage, once said "forgive them Father for they know not what they do".

Easy? Nope!! Doable? Yep (Philippians 4:13) *"For I can do everything through Christ, who gives me strength"*. My key life scripture. What's yours?

So, what I sense my inner spirit saying is that sometimes when folks seem toxic that it just may be a plan of the Lord leading to reconciliation. Desperation is a motivator to look to God. He has been known to work backwards and opposite of earthly wisdom (just ask Gideon, David, Elijah, Paul, and Peter, to name a few).

Graham Cooke says, "He allows with His wisdom what He could easily prevent with His power". This is my favorite of all Graham's wisdom because it helps explain the mystery. The Truth is that, I don't completely understand God's decision, at times, but I do believe in His ultimate goodness. When the decision I was asking Him for did not come, I quickly run to His hiding place and abide.

I realize that this discourse will not wipe out any sadness and concern about your future. We DO have a soul (mind, will and emotions). The Good News is that our Lord sees the end from the beginning and knows His plan.

STAND on THAT and ....

PROCLAIM ALOUD; "JESUS, I WILL NEVER GIVE UP"

God is Big enough to understand our suffering, Wise enough to allow it and Powerful enough to use it for a greater GOOD. But remember, even in Romans 8:28, God is the only one who defines "good". He defines 'good' from His heavenly perspective. But we can trust Him, right? This is why I placed this reminder at the bottom of each day's message saying, "It is not essential to understand everything, but it is essential that we trust God in everything".

"It is not essential that we understand everything,
but that we trust God in everything".

A MOST IMPORTANT TRUTH

Y ou may be asking by now, "When is he going to change topics from the spirit life"? Answer? I don't know. What I DO know is that life in the spirit is the <u>single most important matter</u> for the believer. Why you ask? It is the force that provides a fruitful, healthy life in this season. This Holy Spirit Power is something you cannot manufacture. It is a gift from God.

In fact, when our spirit finally gets in control of our soul, amazing fruit WILL come forth. Our spirit is given to us so that we have a way to relate to God, who Himself is Spirit. We're made in His image. Relationship with God is what the Bible calls life.

Here's the process: Life flows out of our spirit and into our mortal bodies. Before, we were living in the opposite flow. We lived opposite of what creates joy and peace. The only way to live victoriously is through our spirit life and that life is energized by our intimate relationship with the Father as we abide in His presence. I know, it may sound like I am setting some "bar", some "measure", some "achievement" we must obtain to have this intimacy. The fact is that there is a direct relationship between the time we devote to sitting with the Lord and the vitality of our spirit life. I love the "bar" being Jesus.

Chew on this scripture today: John 16:5-13 (NLT) *"But now I am going away to the One who sent me, and not one of you is asking where I am going. Instead, you grieve because of what I've told you. But in fact, it is best for you that I go away, because if I don't, the Advocate won't come. If I do go away, then I will send Him to you. And when He comes, He will convict the world of its sin, and of God's righteousness, and of the coming judgment. The world's sin is that it refuses to believe in Me. Righteousness is available because I go to the Father, and you will see Me no more. Judgement will come because the ruler of this world has already been judged.   There is so much more I want to tell you, but you can't bear it now. When the Spirit of truth comes, He will guide you into all truth.   He will not speak on His own but will tell you what He has heard.   He will tell you about the future".*

Have a God-focused day.

"It is not essential that we understand everything,
but that we trust God in everything".

DAY 17

FAITH VS. FEELINGS

Let's talk about the difference between faith and feelings. We said that God created us so that our faith will rule our life and our feelings. Graham Cooke says, "faith is cold-blooded and has no emotion attached to it". That means we can believe something even if we can't see it or feel it (Hebrews 11:1-3). Many times we are prisoners to our feelings, and emotions as we allow them to rule our thinking and behavior. But in God's order, they exist to serve us so that we may honor God and those around us as well.

I'm going to write out two prayers. The first will come out of the soul and the second from the spirit-led life. Experience the difference by reading them aloud.

Our soul prays, "Father, **I** ask that you will strengthen **me** by your Spirit enabling **me** to overcome **my** weaknesses so that **I** can fight and breakthrough this circumstance." (Notice the references to oneself).

The spirit prays, "Father thank **You** that in my weakness, **You** are my strength. I submit to **Your** rule. *Lord be my strength, live in me and overcome me with **Your** power. Inhabit these circumstances so that **You** will be glorified". (Notice the God references as He becomes the center of the prayer).

As we are dominated by the Spirit in us, we begin to be more considerate, open-hearted and generous because those are the traits of the Father. We are tenderized toward humility.

The Holy Spirit has one agenda for us, and that is that we come under His influence as He continues to reveal Himself. As you can see, that's a good thing.

Let's not be dominated by fear, logic and reason which is earthbound, but rather be dominated by the supernatural kindness and purpose of the Lord Jesus.

KEY: Hide our lives in the Holy Spirit; be wrapped up in Jesus (Psalm 91:1). Don't first look at the circumstances but rather step back and look at God (Matthew 6:33). God is always ready, always prepared to be, for you, exactly what you need. He has already made the deposit (His Spirit). All you need to do is make the withdrawal.

I encourage you to practice these withdrawals in times of need. God loves to 'show off' who He is.

"It is not essential that we understand everything,
but that we trust God in everything".

DAY 18

ACTIVE FAITH

What is faith? Is it trust, or belief, or confidence or what?

To repeat, faith is described in Hebrews 11:1 (NLT). *"Faith shows the reality of what is hoped for; it is the evidence of things we cannot see"*.

Let's break it down. Hebrews says, "reality of what we hope for", which means totally confident, no doubt and self assured in who God is for us. It means being comfortable and at ease with something. What? Comfortable in our hopes for the future. Now isn't the future what we are the most uncomfortable about? So that's the point. Faith is being confident and at ease with the premises of the promises and truths of God. Faith has little to do with intellect or reason. Faith is being assured of the hopes within. Why? Because if we have an intimate relationship with God, we must believe that it was HE that put the hopes there in the first place. I just heard Rush Limbaugh say in regard to life's employment pursuits, "...discover what your passion is and jump in head first with all the gusto you have". History has proven that it works more times than it doesn't. We are best at what we love and it's much easier too, because we are self-motivated.

Next, faith is believing evidence that we have yet to see. What? This is getting crazier, right? No wonder faith-filled people often appear to be different. How can we see evidence of something we have yet to see? I'm not sure, but it could have to do with believing that you have heard from the Lord (in the many ways that can happen), and moving out on 'that' basis. I once believed that I heard God say to resign being pastor of the church I served. Later, with confirmations from my wife, I did. Weeks later, I was introduced to Commission To Every Nation. As I write, I have served there 18 years. So how does one acquire more faith to live like that? I believe that when you accept Christ, you get

ALL of Him and His Spirit. We ALWAYS have enough of Him. It's just practicing what we believe, even if we may look a little silly. We simply appropriate what we already have within us and move out with active faith.

Now what is "active faith"? Active faith is not feelings or work-based. Some days we may feel faithless, so we speak a prayer USING God's promises to get us going. On other days, we are big on faith, so we work with assurance of our belief. Don't have faith in your faith (you may have to read this more than once). We have faith in only one thing, or better stated, One person and that's the Lord God Almighty, Jesus His Son, and His Holy Spirit.

Active faith is being strategically connected to the Father, who is the head of His church. He called it His body. Faith is NOT something to be mastered; rather, it is something to accept and walk in because it is what and who we are. In Hebrews 11:6, we read, "…it is impossible to please God without faith." We are kids of the King and co-heirs in the Kingdom. We have all the authority we will ever need.

Bottom line: Faith comes from only one source. It comes from having a deep relationship with the Father, because of Jesus and by His Holy Spirit. Faith is a bit weird, not reasonable at times, but the 'confidence' comes from believing that the Lord is THE faithful One. (Revelation 19:11). The evidence comes through three sources. One, is the Word; two, is the God-testimony of others; and three, is your own experience (yes you DO have experiences that prove His faithfulness). Go now and release Active Faith.

"It is not essential that we understand everything,
but that we trust God in everything".

DAY 19

NOTHING IS IMPOSSIBLE FOR ME

Faith means that you link your impossibilities to God's possibilities. Jeremiah 32:27 says: "I am the Lord of all peoples of the world. Is anything too hard for me"? In Luke 18:27 Jesus reminds us saying, "What is impossible for people is possible with God".

Yes, we've heard these statements before but, we may say, "my experiences don't verify it." However, our problem is that Jesus tells us the truth. The good news is that Jesus Christ wants to bless your life as you reach out to Him in faith. By not reaching out, you may miss the blessing.

Even the prophet, as recorded in Jeremiah 32:17, stated the truth about God saying, "Nothing is too hard for You". Why? I think it was to remind others what God can do. We must deeply desire the power to overcome the impossible. We could call it faith-power. Example: Today we have just learned during staff prayer time that a child with Downs Syndrome has been totally healed. Really!!

We should <u>desire</u> God's best, so that we can <u>acquire</u> His best, so that we might <u>be</u> His best.

This is how it works: Jesus saves us and makes us His partners. He redeems us and sends us out as His messengers. And, as we seek Him, He enriches us that we might be capable ambassadors, representative of His way, truth and lifestyle.

Robert Schuller said, "The secret of success is to find a need and fill it; to find a hurt and heal it; and to find somebody with a problem and offer to help solve it." That is what is called mission.

We are on a mission, empowered by the Sender, to do His good works. There are only two kinds of Christians. Those that are sent out and those who send. Most members of the church are senders and without them, missionaries like my wife and me, could not survive to do His work full time.

Let's say together ALOUD: I am able because God in me is able. I am created in His image and nothing, absolutely nothing, is impossible as the Lord gives the release. Nothing is impossible for me because nothing is impossible for God in me.

"It is not essential that we understand everything, but that we trust God in everything".

DAY 20

FAITH CAN BRING PEACE

Let's hear it again. Hebrews 11:1, "Faith shows the reality of what we hope for, it is the evidence of things we cannot see". It's not intellectual, but it is true. Having faith is to be sure of your hope. What 'hope' is the writer talking about? Well, the author goes on to tell about some of the heroes of the Bible. He showed how their faith made what they did possible. Then in Hebrews 11: 29 and 30, the author tells us that even though they have a great demonstration of faith, they did not see what God promised. We discover that faith is not about a result; rather, it is a lifestyle. We live by faith so that we are available to the Lord for His use and purpose but not for what we can get out of it. Faith is our genuine response to God's goodness and gifts.

It's interesting that in Romans 8:25, Paul says the same thing. "But if we hope for what we do not see, we eagerly wait for it with perseverance". Biblical hope is nonsense to the world of reason and intellectual thinking. However, it is everything to the believer. Paul says, "We are to 'eagerly' wait for God's promises even if it takes endurance". We are to "hang in there". So what's the alternative? I think it is doing it on our own ahead of His good purpose and intention. So how's that working for you?

In Romans 8:26-30, Paul goes on to reassure us as to how all this works. Just how do we keep on keeping on when nothing "seems" to be happening? Well, we pray in the Spirit and when we do, He intercedes for us, leading us to the way God wants it to be. I believe that verse 26 validates our spiritual prayer language and one of its purposes. When we don't know how or what to pray in our own language, we speak in a spiritual language or even just 'groan'. His Holy Spirit, who searches our heart, knows exactly what to do with our prayers. Is that comforting or what? We are not required to offer intellectual, impressive prayers. He is just waiting for us to offer a humble prayer. Hasn't God made this easy?

I remind you again of the scripture that many know as Romans 8:28, where Paul says that *"all things work for the good for those who love God and are called according to His purpose"*. I translate that to mean that everything that God sends or allows to engage our lives, comes with His permission and for His purposes. My response is to say, "Thanks, Lord, for this. Now what do I do with it"?

Actually, if we will live life like this, the result will be peace. Maybe even a "peace that passes understanding". And what is the purpose? In Romans 8:29, the purpose is to become like Jesus. We are to live, work and treat others just like Jesus did. And it's possible, folks. Peace comes from trusting God and relaxing in His purposes. Joy is the result of our released peace.

Bottom line: If God is for us (and He is) then who can be against us with any real effectiveness?

"It is not essential that we understand everything,
but that we trust God in everything".

DAY 21

LIFE SHOULD BE A FAITH WALK

There's an old saying, "Life's a cake walk." I'm not sure what that really means but it could refer to the "cake walk" at school carnivals (back in the old days). People would buy a ticket and then stand in a circle on squares with numbers. Music would start, folks would walk around the circle and when it stopped, a number would be called. If it was the number square you were standing on, you would get the cake. So one meaning of the saying might be that in life, sometimes you win but most of the time you don't. In either case, you have to pay. In other words, life's a gamble.

Well, I prefer the truth. Life's a faith walk. Your life's perspective depends upon what you choose as a foundation for your faith. Most choose to place their faith in themselves, others, institutions or the lottery (what some call luck). So if that describes you, how's it working for ya? Of course, I don't believe that describes you, right?

It doesn't take long for us to realize that trusting ourselves or others usually comes up lacking. We may try to do our best but life's challenges often times surpass our skill level (check out Proverbs 3:5; 1 Corinthians 7:5; John 5:30). When we try institutions, we often learn that they lean more toward preserving the institution than those they serve. Institutional integrity is only as good as the people who lead them. And then there's luck. Two of the synonyms are "chance" and accident". Yeah, that's what I want to do, live my life trusting chance and accidental fortune.

Truthfully, I must correct a previous statement. Ultimately, it's not "what" you have faith in. It's "who". Faith is the most important topic in the Bible. There is documentary called Is Genesis History, that provides scientific proof of earth's creation in six 24 hour days. Check it out on Youtube. Yet, Genesis was not written to give us science about how the earth was created; rather it tells us Who created it and for whom He created it. The story of scripture reveals the nature and character of God and how He deals with His creation. It is a story of the importance of relationships, both vertical (divine) and horizontal (people). It is a manual on how these relationships are to be established and developed. It is a guide to unveiling God's plan of ruling the earth by delegating His authority and power to His people on the earth.

For a while, we are going to talk about faith because it is at the core of our relationship with Father. To restate that, the Bible says in Hebrews 11:6, "...*it is impossible to please God without faith*". So, I'm guessing we should develop our faith life.

"Anyone who wants to come to Him, must believe that God exists and that he rewards those who sincerely seek Him. (Hebrews 11:6) We MUST believe that the Jesus in us is greater than our #1 enemy, who is in the world. In fact, I will prove it as we move forward. For today, find some faith in God or the 'God Kind of faith', and hold on to it.

"It is not essential that we understand everything,
but that we trust God in everything".

DAY 22

ENOUGH FAITH

The Bible is clear about a believer's faith. Each of us has faith. As we read in Ephesians 2:8, "by grace you have been saved through faith; it is a gift from God". Romans 12 tells us that the Lord, in His ultimate wisdom, gave each of us a measure of faith. So quit saying, "I just don't have faith", because it simply isn't true. Romans 10:8 tells us that the Word of God is called the Word of Faith. Scripture is faith food.

Each believer has the same amount of Jesus in them. He didn't give me 62% of Himself and you 33%. We all work for an equal opportunity employer. We don't "need" faith; we simply need to appropriate what is already in us. This will be a test of our premise: **our faith over feelings, His truth over confusion, and our belief over experience**. One thing I know is this: the Word of God is true all the time. His Word is the only true source of reality. Jesus tells us in Matthew 4:4 that, *"People do not live by bread alone, but by every* word *that comes out of the mouth of God"*. Scripture builds our faith. Faith relies on scripture. Eternal truth is found in scripture.

So each of us has some faith and it is enough to do what God needs of us. Jesus said, all you need is faith the size of a mustard seed (one of the smallest seeds of His day) and you can move a mountain (Matthew 17:20). So if you never choose to do anything to grow your faith beyond your allotted measure, you have enough right now to do greater things. But it must be possible to grow your faith because we hear biblical references to "little faith, great faith, and full of faith". So what do you do? I assume that you are on a quest for more of God in more of you. In fact, I have discovered that a powerful prayer is simply, "More, God."

So, let's begin to act on what we have. Someone said, let's not worry about doing the "greater things" as Jesus prophesied, but let's just begin to do what they did in the book of Acts. Let's use the measure we now possess. Let's start to act like a child of God endowed with His capabilities. What do you have faith for right now? Do that. If you're not ready to pray for a serious illness to be healed, how about a headache? If you're not ready to speak against your fear and have it totally removed, how about speaking to the moment, the current fear? Try this prayer, "I declare I have the power of God. I decree this fear I have, to be removed, in Jesus' name."

We feed on the Word to build our faith and then we must act on it or it has been nothing but an intellectual exercise. Having faith is not so we can merely 'feel good'. Possessing faith is so that we can be God's ambassadors of the Good News. The Good News that we are free from thinking small; that we are free to express extravagant kindness; that we are free to immediately forgive a wrong; that we are free to be amazing with generosity; that we are free to not be offended and that we are free to extend His supernatural hand to see people blessed.

Sometimes we believe in a *small* God, when in fact, He is WAY out of our box. Our experience seems to tell us that faith stuff just doesn't work and we should look to the "big boys and girls" in the Christian celebrity spotlight to do the works of God. But if you will listen to their story and to their history, you will see they all started with what they had and acted out in belief of what the Bible tells us about who we really are. For instance, we are: 'God's heirs, together with Christ' (Romans 8:17; Galatians 3:29 and 4:7; Titus 3:7). *"we are filled up with the fullness of God* "(Ephesians 3:19), *"we are His masterpiece created in Christ Jesus for good works"* (Ephesians 2:10). Why? In John 17:21 Jesus said, that "(we) *may all be 'one', just as you and I are one, You are in me, Father and I am in you"*. And that they be in Us so that the world might believe You send me".

Bottom Line: You have enough faith. You have sufficient faith to do His work. So what's next?

"It is not essential that we understand everything,
but that we trust God in everything".

MOVING MOUNTAINS

Faith: (my paraphrase) "It is the confident assurance that what we hope for is going to happen. It is the evidence of things we have yet to see". The fundamental fact of our existence is that this trust in God, this faith, is the firm foundation under everything that makes life worth living. It's our handle on what we can't see". What? Well, that's scripture for you. The writer of Hebrews 11:1, inspired by the mind of God, gives us a definition of faith. But does it help?

You see, faith is of the heart, not the head. Faith is not intellectual, rather intuitive from within. In fact, in my 41+ years of pastoral experience, those who seem to have the greatest difficulty with faith are the intellectuals. Well, I don't know about you, but that gives me great hope.

So what is "heart" when we see it in the scriptures? In the original languages (Hebrew, Aramaic, Greek) it meant 'inward, concealed, thoughts, feelings and middle or center'. But listen to KJV translation of 1 Peter 3:4, "let it be the hidden man of the heart which is not corruptible, an adornment of the meek (humble) and quiet spirit". It appears to me that 'heart', here, relates to our Jesus-filled spirit located in the very center of our being. It is an imperishable, incorruptible quality and is called a "quiet spirit". Makes sense. Our spirit cannot be polluted by outside forces for it has the very nature of God's Holy Spirit mixed in it.

In Mark 11:23, we read that if you speak to a mountain, without a doubt in your heart to be thrown into the sea, it will happen. What's your current 'mountain'? We can have doubts in our soul (mind, will, emotions) but not in our incorruptible spirit. Paul teaches, "for it is by believing in your heart that you are made right with God..." Later Paul would say *"though our bodies are dying, our spirit (inward man of the heart) is being renewed every day"*. (2 Corinthians 4:16). We communicate with the physical world with our physical senses, but we communicate with the spiritual world with our spirit. It seems that your Christian life must be led by your spirit, not your soul. In fact, the role of the Spirit is to rule your soul so that your mind, will and emotions reflect Jesus.

Faith seems to be built as we step out into the realms of the "conviction of things not seen". <u>Faith is not understanding something, rather it is doing something you understand.</u> It was one thing for Peter, who was in the boat, to say to Jesus, tell me to come to You on the water, but quite another to put full weight on the water. In the story told in Matthew 14:22-33, apparently, it was Peter's belief that enabled him to ask Jesus to call him out of the boat, but it was faith that allowed him to put his full weight on the raging water. And you know what, it worked. Now did Peter, that great apostle, have more of Jesus than you? What's the difference? Maybe Peter got in touch with his spirit at that moment. Oh yeah, later Peter couldn't find enough faith to confess he even knew Jesus, while Jesus was being falsely accused at his trial. So, he denied knowing Him three times. But I must say that overall, Peter was amazing. He did get out of the boat and later died a martyr's death proclaiming Christ. In fact, his troubling moments alongside his powerful witness, gives me courage.

Remember, I said that "life's a faith walk", so keep those boots walking.

"It is not essential that we understand everything,
but that we trust God in everything".

DAY 24

WRAPPING FAITH AROUND BELIEF

Proverbs 3:5 states (Amplified) *"Lean on, trust and be confident in the Lord with all your heart and mind, and do not rely on your own insight and understanding."* We said that doubting the ability of God to do something can impede His action in your behalf. Being double minded is something we all have faced, yet we read in James 1:6, *"But when you ask Him be sure that your faith is in God alone. Do not waver; for a person with divided loyalty is as unsettled as a wave of the sea that is blown and tossed by the wind"*.

That's what we saw as recorded in John 20:24, as the apostle Thomas confronted his fellow apostles saying that he would not believe the Lord had risen from the dead unless he saw the nail holes in his hands and side. Whoops! Better watch what words come out of our mouths for we may soon eat them. It's interesting that when confronted with the reality of the risen Lord, Thomas made a confession; but it wasn't what we'd call a "confession of faith" because Jesus was there up close and personal. And notice that Jesus didn't recommend the Thomas 'kind of faith'. Jesus said, yeah, Thomas you believe because you saw but, *"blessed are those that will believe who have never seen Me"* (John 20:29). In other words, He is saying, I love it when people act on faith rather than sight when it comes to following Me.

Faith is a present tense kind of thing not a future tense. When God spoke to Abram in Genesis 17 saying that the 99-year-old man would have a son by his barren 90-year-old wife, he believed the Lord on what was spoken rather on what logic would tell him or needing a vision to "prove" it. Not only that, the Lord told him he would be the father of nations. What, at 99 years of age? Impossible!

We too, must take a stand on what has been spoken in the Word and by the still small voice of God within us. Mostly in the past, I have stood on what I saw, experienced or felt. But today, I'm moved on what I believe no matter how crazy that sounds to others, particularly other Christians. Some say, 'well, I'll believe it when I see it". Well, do you believe you have brains? Ever see them?

We serve a God who calls things that are 'not', as if they 'were'. Romans 4:17 teaches that our God, who gives life to the dead, and speaks of non-existent things as if they already existed, does so in confidence of Who He is. Also Paul says Abraham became a father because Abraham believed. We serve a God that is so huge that it is impossible to get our mind around His capabilities and yet we can get our faith around it. I encourage you to agree with what is already written in the Bible as a testimony to who He is and what He will do. It is said that we can be absolutely sure of who God is, yet not so sure about how, or when, He will do what He wants to do.

KEY: As much as we can at any moment, we must completely trust the Lord's wisdom and leadership as we live on earth. Life gets very simple if you trust Him as much and as often as possible. Whatever is happening in you right now, the one and only God who called Himself, "I AM" is with you. He is totally confident in what He wants to do. It's vital that we remain child-like in His presence for it's the only way we can mature in our faith. I know, that's a paradox. Be a child so you can mature. Who but God could think like that?

"It is not essential that we understand everything,
but that we trust God in everything".

DAY 25

FAITH ASKS, 'WHAT DO I DO?'

This morning, my scripture reading was Luke 17. Within that chapter, the apostles were asking Jesus, "increase our faith" to which He responded, "if you had faith (confidence in God) even as small as a mustard seed, you could even say to this mulberry tree, May you be uprooted and thrown into the sea and it would obey you". (Luke 17:6).

Makes perfect sense? Not really, but it is the Word authored by God Himself and given to Luke. "Well, it was just a metaphor, an illustration for describing the power of God", you'd say. Yeah, but remember ole Phillip the evangelist? In Acts 8, he was evangelizing and healing and causing a stir among the people when God told him to leave (right in the middle of a revival) and go toward Gaza. He obeyed (good example for us) and the Lord led him to witness to an Ethiopian official and then baptize him. Cool, right? But wait. <u>Suddenly</u>, Phillip found himself at Azotus: which was miles away. He was a real live demonstration of Luke 17's mulberry tree as he was supernaturally transported by the spoken word of God in an instant. The scripture actually says, "...the Spirit of the Lord snatched Philip away." (Acts 8:39).

Why do I tell you this? To show that no matter how wild the Word of God sounds to you, He can be trusted to follow through and is capable of doing so. Deuteronomy 29:29 tells us that the "secret things" belong to God, but the things which are revealed, belong to us. I choose to live with God on a 'need to know' basis, and I love it that way. What He wants to keep 'secret', He will, and when He chooses to give us a Rhema (spoken) word, He will. I'll take all He gives and leave the rest to His wisdom. Can you think of times in your life where God chose not to give you the whole story because if He had, you might have chickened out? He also knows when you are NOT ready for His future in the present moment. Praise God for His wisdom, right?

So why are we not seeing "signs and wonders" in our lives? I plead Deuteronomy 29:29 and Isaiah 55:8-9. (Read, I'll wait) But the Bible gives a hint at one possibility in Mark 11:25-26. Unforgiveness can interfere with your faith and the release of the power of God in you. If you are having a problem breaking through, go here first. Ask the Holy Spirit, if there is any bitterness, towards anyone with whom you hold a grudge? Is there anyone you have not forgiven for a wrong? Is there anyone that even when you see them, your "skin crawls" (an indication that bitterness reigns)? You might want to take care of business. If you've offended anyone you must forgive them. Yes, even if you believe you were 100% in the right, forgive, because the offense still stands in your heart and needs release. Now, if you ask them to forgive you, they don't have to accept it. I've had that happen to me but when I left, I felt clean and at peace. Offering forgiveness frees us of bondage to the wound of pain and hurt. We may not forget, but we can remember with a peaceful heart.

Generally, I encourage you not to spend much time trying to figure out why God is not doing something you have requested and within the time you have requested. Just don't go there. Never ask why! Ask, "what do I need to do here, Lord?"

Wisdom tells me that if you want to be better, be quick to repent, quick to forgive and be genuine when you do. God will NOT accept 'religious' acts of piety. But He is a God of his Word. When He says something, it is the Truth. My favorite name for God is in Revelation 19:11 where He is called, "Faithful and True." What we think about God is the most important thing in the world. How we perceive Him will dictate how we live. Is He big enough? Is He faithful enough? Is He powerful enough? Is He forgiving enough? Answer: "Yes, yes, yes, yes and yes".

"It is not essential that we understand everything,
but that we trust God in everything".

DAY 26

FAITH IS EMPOWERED
BY WILLINGNESS

Faith is a principle that <u>requires</u> us to act on what we believe. Faith is not an intellectual issue but rather a matter of the heart. Faith is not automatic. The power of God in us does not flow just because we believe but rather because we act. We live out what we believe. One must do more than simply sit and believe. God, in His great design, has called us into partnership to enact His purposes. We are His hands and feet on earth.

In the story recorded in Ezekiel 20:5-6, the Bible says if we will be willing and obedient, we will eat the good of the land. So, what's that? When God created the heavens and the earth as recorded in Genesis 1, He defined what was 'good'. He'd say, "*let there be light and there was light. And God saw that the light was good*". Jesus was speaking to a rich young man in Mark 10:18 who called Him "good teacher". Jesus answered, "*Why do you call me good? No one is good except God alone*". In effect, He was saying you must think I'm God to call me good. My point? God is the one who defines the 'good' of the land. One thing I'm sure of is that if we are willing and obedient, we'll taste His goodness.

KEY: <u>Willingness</u> and <u>obedience</u> are fundamental to activating the faith within us. Faith works in all of our lives; spiritual, physical, mental, financial and emotional. In Psalm 50:10-11, (NASB) God describes His dominion. "*Every beast of the forest is Mine, the cattle on a thousand hills. I know every bird of the mountains and everything that moves is Mine. The world is Mine and all it contains.*" Then the Apostle John reminds us in 1 John 5:14 (NASB), "*and this is the boldness which we have toward him, that if we ask anything according to his will, He hears* *us.*" He is simply asking us, encouraging us to ask in faith based on Who He is and what He wants for us, His kids.

God is saying, "Know my will for you and <u>just do it</u>". See, Nike wasn't the first with that slogan.

But you say, "How do I know His will?" I think He would answer, "I have already revealed it to you and I am constantly (24/7) trying to guide you in it." So why do we feel we don't know His will? It could be many things, such as not knowing what He has already told us in His word. Or it may just be (this is my problem) that my self-will blots out His directives. Another possibility is we think that just because we are saved that we can automatically know day to day what He wants. But it's NOT automatic. We are required to participate, to engage. It may be that you are putting off committing to a dedicated time to sit with Him and under Him. By the way, it appears that Jesus did this daily on His earth-bound journey.

If your holy intentions were sincere and graced by His will, it would move you out of conviction into action. God is the best steward ever. He gives us the opportunity to be used for 'good' purposes. We are being transformed in our spirit so that we can be POWERFULLY used for His 'good' pleasure. The result of our inward journey is an outward action. That outward action can transform another.

It's a Good thing!

Paul put it this way in Romans 12:1-2 NASB, "*Be transformed by the renewing of your mind that you may prove what the will of God is, that which is good and acceptable.*" The rest of that chapter talks about how our faith-walk affects the people around us. Moving out in faith is not about us, but about others who benefit from our lifestyle examples of God's love and kindness. What a wonderful life. So let's share it.

"It is not essential that we understand everything,
but that we trust God in everything".

FAITH REQUIRED PERSISTENCE

Having faith is not just about you. Within God's economy, faith should extend to others. Some are not at the point of faith that you are and it is at those times where you can extend your faith to cover them. We just ask if they will agree with us about the matter of their heart and then enact the, *"where two agree"* principle and speak it forth to bless them. This principle is found in Jesus' comments in Matthew 18:19-20. (Read it now, I'll wait).

We must believe that God IS the God described in the Bible. When we speak a word of faith according to the scriptures, we are believing God for it. And as we've said, belief must move from our head to our inner being that the Bible sometimes calls the 'heart'. Faith is taking the facts of the truth from the Word and putting them into action. It's not about what we 'feel' or 'think' because we can't work ourselves up to it. It's about what God said and what God did as demonstrated in the Bible. Then you, standing on <u>that</u> truth, can speak the truth in love.

In Genesis 15, the Lord said, "Then Abram believed the Lord, and the Lord counted him as righteous because of his faith". He will regard the faith you have, His gift to you, as the basis of His approval of you. Notice, I did <u>not</u> say His approval is based on your use of your faith. He knows it is our faith that connects us to Him. Jesus said, Matthew 11:6, *"Whoever doesn't lose his faith in Me is indeed blessed."* You see how important faith is to God? Jesus encourages us, Matthew 21:22, *"Have faith that you will receive whatever you ask for in prayer."* But he also warns us, Matthew 24:10, "Then many will lose faith. They will betray and hate each other."

Again in Matthew 15, Jesus is confronted by a woman who wanted her daughter healed. She kept on asking and asking, really not giving up because she knew what He could do. Her daughter's health was that important to her. Ultimately, He said, "Woman, your (persistent) faith, is great, your request is granted." Do we give up too soon on that which the scripture is clear? Can we believe that he can provide even though we don't see it happening at the moment? Wonder what we've missed out on? Let us miss out no longer.

We will go on to other matters but FAITH will always be in there somewhere. Like a computer program running behind the scenes but always available, so will faith be in my future writings. Like Jesus in John 16:1, I too say, "*I have said these things to you so that you won't lose your faith.*" The fact is that you can't really lose what God has given but you can ignore it. Don't!

"It is not essential that we understand everything,
but that we trust God in everything".

DAY 28

OUR WORK IN THE JOURNEY

One of my ultimate goals is to self-rule. The Bible, in Galatians 5, calls it "self-control" as a fruit of the Spirit. A believers' self-rule begins at the cross. The true Word of the cross is what Jesus said in Mark 14:36, "....Everything is possible for you (Father). Please take this cup of suffering away from Me. Yet, I want Your will to be done, not Mine." Of course, these are the words Jesus spoke to His Father right before He KNEW He would be betrayed and killed. This makes these words even more significant. Graham Cooke says that the only form of control that is acceptable in the church or between people is self control.

A self-governed person chooses to submit their soul to their spirit. This is key. I am currently a work in progress toward this reachable goal. The question I am asking in the situations of my life is, "Is what I am thinking of, just said or done, all about me? It needs to be all about YOU, Lord." How do we think like this? Think God first in all things, which is what I believe Jesus was saying in Matthew 6:33.

This framework for living life daily gives us a different perspective on stuff and folks. Am I mad at (name)? Why? Is it all about me? Is it all about what I want, how I think things should be? Am I putting a person into my world and expecting them to respond as I would respond to them? This can result in unnegotiated expectations. I've learned that unnegotiated expectations can turn into an offense towards others. My favorite saying is that expectations can become premeditated resentments.

In Jesus' world, it is always about the Father. Jesus often said, (my paraphrase), "I just do what I see the Father doing and say what I hear the Father saying". How? Because He daily stayed close to the Father.

Ultimately, this will mean thinking God not just during your devotional times but at 10:00am and 1:14pm, and 6:41pm, all throughout your day.

Now this takes work, and it is part of the sacred journey. I believe that if you will take to heart what I am saying, you will pass me up in spiritual depth in no time. Many of you are already ahead of where I was at your age, I promise.

Meditate on this today; I believe Jesus would say to us today, "All who love me will do what I say. My Father will love them and We will come and make Our home with each of them." Isn't that awesome!

"It is not essential that we understand everything,
but that we trust God in everything".

DAY 29

GOD LIKES TO BE PURSUED

Ephesians 1:9-10 says, "God has now revealed to us his mysterious will regarding Christ, which is to fulfill His own good plan. And this is the plan. At the right time, He will bring everything together under the authority of Christ, everything in heaven and on earth."

It's all about Jesus. The ultimate purpose of God is to sum up all things in His son. Our ultimate purpose is to be conformed to the image of Christ. We need to know the image of Jesus Christ. One of the best ways I have found is "read the Red". In some bibles, Jesus' words are printed in red. (search "the Red Letters" in Amazon.com). This is why it is so important for us to become intimate with the Father. The more we are, the more we will know what Jesus is about. The more we know what Jesus is about, the simpler life becomes. I didn't say easy, just simpler. I'll take simple all day long.

Rick Joyner wrote a piece that states what we've been talking about in these Daily Upgrades. Rick says, "Jesus loves to draw us to Him. He may do that with enticing mysteries that grab our attention, or He may do so by calamity and difficulty, where it's God or nothing, or He may do that by His kindness which calls for a thanksgiving response. Bottom line is that He is a God that likes to be pursued. Those who pursue Him will find Him. It's probably based upon the earthly principle that we spend whatever it takes pursuing what we really care about. If He is really our first love, He will be our primary life pursuit." Thanks, Rick.

All I can do is encourage you to stay after Him. Don't give up simply because you have been lax or think you have failed. I promise you that this pursuit is worth all you give to it.

You cannot fail the Lord. On the cross, He paid for all your future failures. But there are times we "take a break" or not live up to His way, truth and life. No problem, as we, who have done those things, are still in His family. But the Lord loves you for who you are right now, not for what you should be. His heart is to love you into where He wants you to be. Read the famous story of the prodigal (imprudent) son recorded in Luke 15:11-32. It is rich.

Pursuit (the Bible calls this perseverance) is the key element of Daily Upgrades. I promise that this pursuit of the One who loves you <u>no matter what</u>, is worth all you have to give.

KEY: Start with willful discipline and wait for God to transform your heart's effort into a desire.

"It is not essential that we understand everything,
but that we trust God in everything".

DAY 30

KIDS OF THE OVERCOMER

We <u>will not</u> let our mutual enemy ruin our destiny that is authorized by our loving Father in Heaven. We WILL NOT. In a 'time' of persecution, we will know how to live in the "secret place" (Psalm 91) of the Lord God Almighty. Let us be keenly sensitive and aware of these "times" as opportunities to use all of our God-given authority to stand against the so called "flaming arrows" of the enemy (Ephesians 6:16). Jesus said He is an overcomer and later told us that with His authority and permission, we will do even greater things than He did. So, we too, are overcomers in each moment as we activate the power of God for goodness sake. We are Kids of the Overcomer.

This will take a conscious, willful effort on our part for it will be natural for us to slip into our "usual" mode of soulish thinking and ultimately soulish acting. This is driven by fear and sustained by our ignorance of the spiritual power deposited in us, through the Holy Spirit. We are being taught to simply speak it as if it had already happened (Mark 11:22-23). As Paul said, ("be strong in the Lord and in His mighty power (Ephesians 6:10)." Who's strength? Who's power? We step back, call on the Lord, speak boldly what is our desire, and watch Him work.

I'm telling you, we are stepping into a new season, a new time, where all the capability and wisdom and power of the Lord is available to you – yes, you! (Of course, it always has been). Now we know and because of that, we can use our Godly resources at will. It's ok to call on others to stand with you. Actually, it's biblically stated in Matthew 18:19 *"if two of you agree on earth about anything, it shall be done for them by My Father in Heaven"* (Matthew 18:19). Our part is to agree together and His part is to do it as it fits into His specific will. Who's the power agent here, us or <u>God</u>? Who's the originator here, us or <u>God</u>? (Obvious answer is <u>underlined</u>).

God is not going to take away every life challenge, but He is going to give revelation. God is not going to allow us to avoid all difficulty. It's the very way we are encouraged by His provision. In our joyful dependency, we can live expectantly. If we are to learn to be overcomers, we must allow ourselves to be developed from the inside out. It's always our choice that leads to His trustworthiness to grow our faith.

Pausing in the midst of challenge, taking a breath, literally or figuratively, stepping back, and looking up to Father-God's wisdom is what I call a Daily Upgrade.

His faithfulness (Revelation 19:11) tells me that He is always available. However, to get an upgrade of faith and joy, we do have to act. That is our agreed partnership with the Lord. My heart says you can do this, one day at a time.

"It is not essential that we understand everything,
but that we trust God in everything".

DAY 31

BONUS

I came across three sayings and have not discovered who wrote them. Nevertheless, they made me think. Do we make the spiritual quest too complicated? Can it be more simple?

Here's what I found on Pintrest.com: "Man says…Show me and I will trust You. God says…Trust Me and I will show you"; "LISTEN and SILENT are spelled with the same letters"; and "There are times that we really don't understand God. But guess what? We are not asked to understand God. Only to trust. We call it faith". Maybe this spiritual quest is not so complicated.

As we sit before the Father in our time 'behind the shut door' (Mt.6:6), we may want an 'outpouring' from Him and we want it NOW. Yet as with the "water to wine" miracle (John 2), the outpouring of water turned the water into wine as it was being poured. What's the principle here? Outpouring happens before the manifestation. Yes, we want the manifestation, but Papa God wants the relationship first. Next, He wants us to actively pour. Faith in the mind is merely an intellectual exercise and that is why the Apostle James (James 2:26) reminded us "faith is dead without works". By saying "dead", I think he meant non-existent. Another example told in 1 Kings 17:10-16 is when the prophet Elijah confronts a poor widow. He tells her to give him bread (during a famine). She replied that she only has a small amount of flour and oil. But as the story unfolds, she never runs out of either resource for three years. It continued to be available as needed, <u>as she poured</u>.

It seems to me that it is all about simple trust in the Supernatural, which is The Super + the natural. Like my friend Max Greiner likes to say, "I do the natural; He does the Supernatural." Our Creator-God put this nature in us. Our grand Designer gave us a spirit so we could become one with His Holy Spirit. This Supernatural experience allows our limited nature to be empowered by His Unlimited Nature. In that combined nature, Big things happen. I think it is awesome to realize that this "Super Substance" of the Holy Spirit was originally designed to be ready and available for release by His Kids from within their unique nature.

How do you hear from your Creator so faith can become an action? It's simple, really. Just desire to want more and continually check in with Him. Next, do your best to ask Him for direction or clarity, at the moment. Questions you might ask would be, "What is this, Father?"; What am I to do here?; and What are You doing here, Lord?".

Truth is that your #1 Lover is eager to be one with you in power. He is simply waiting for you to pour.

Here's your encouragement from Matthew 11:29-30 (MSG) "*Are you tired? Worn out? Burned out on religion? Come to me. Get away with me and you'll recover your life. I'll show you how to take a real rest. Walk with me and work with me—watch how I do it. Learn the unforced rhythms of grace. I won't lay anything heavy or ill-fitting on you. Keep company with me and you'll learn to live freely and lightly.*"

Now my friend, daily go get an Upgrade, Daily.

"It is not essential that we understand everything,
but that we trust God in everything".

About the Author

Jack was born in San Antonio, Texas and enjoyed a healthy upbringing with his sister, M'Lel. He served in the US Army spending 13 months in Vietnam in the mid 1960's.

Jack and Carol have been married over 50 years. She has been his ministry co-laboring partner for over 41 of those years. They have two awesome children and five super-gifted grandkids.

Jack holds a Bachelor degree from East Texas State University and a Master of Divinity degree from Texas Christian University's Brite Divinity School Ft. Worth, Texas.

He has been senior Pastor of three congregations in various places in Texas over a span of 23 years. Those were times of growth and maturation as a pastor and son of The Most High God. He and Carol were blessed to serve caring churches who loved and supported them along the way.

In March of 2000, the Lord spoke simultaneously to Jack and Carol directing them to resign the church in Kerrville, Texas and await their next assignment. They agreed with Father God and stepped into an unknown future leaving the pastorate in June 2000.

Three churches asked Jack to become their pastor but neither he, nor Carol, sensed the go-ahead from the Lord on any of these offers. In late June, Jack was offered a staff position with a newly created mission agency in Kerrville. The challenge was that this offer was a faith-based position, which meant they would have to raise their own salary. Support raising was a new and rather frightening concept.

But, in August 2000, God made it clear that they were to accept the offer and join the staff to develop an arm of the ministry that would provide pastoral care for the growing number of missionaries around the globe. While serving as Director of Pastoral Care, Commission To Every Nation (CTEN) continued to grow both in number of missionary staff and home office staff.

In February 2011, when the mission director resigned, the founder asked Jack to become the Executive Director of the entire mission. He currently serves in that position overseeing 30 home staff, seven full time pastoral care couples and over 725 missionaries in 61 nations.

Serving with an amazing administrative team, Jack and Carol are confident they are right where they need to be. He has learned that hearing God must precede obeying and obedience often must precede understanding all the details. Jack's primary heart is to help others create an intimacy with the Father to be in a position to hear His still, small Voice.

If you are interested in having a conversation about becoming a faith-based missionary, or learning more about how you can create a greater depth of intimacy with your heavenly Father, you are invited to contact Jack for a warm Texas chat.

jackrothenflue@cten.org

www.cten.org

Appendix 1

Why REST?

Sounds simple, right? Immediately, we get this picture of ourselves outside in a hammock, partly sunny 70 degree day with a gentle breeze. We hear the soft sounds of birds chirping and oh yes, we have a cool glass of lemonade to enjoy. It is quiet, serene and peaceful. There is a sign above you that reads, "Don't, even, bother me". Your focus is on the 'peace' with no demands. Yep, I like that and truthfully, we all need some hammock time.

Well to REST (Relaxed Engaged Simple Trusting) does include some of these ingredients. However, to REST in the Lord has a deeper purpose and more significant results. The REST I am suggesting is as ancient as the first Adam, as noted in Genesis. We know that even the Creator, Himself, rested at the conclusion of His wildly creative masterpiece called earth. Was that because He was tired? I think not. I believe He was engaging all that He had fearfully and wonderfully made and called it 'very good'. His highest and best work was creating humanity made in the image of the Father, Son and Holy Spirit. From the beginning, He engaged Adam and Eve in the 'cool of the day'. It seems evident that God loves to talk.

Apparently, REST is important. In fact, we are reminded by the fourth commandment in Exodus 20:8, that we are to have "a day of rest dedicated to the Lord your God" for worship. REST is foundational to worship. To worship is to set time aside for engaging God with respectful praise and thanksgiving. I believe God shows us clearly that this kind of REST is important so that each of His kids will have an opportunity to experience an active dialogue with our Creator.

Many times King David shared ongoing conversations with God during his REST. An example is found in Psalms 12:1 where David says, "Help, O Lord..." to which God replies "...I have seen the violence done to the helpless....now I will rise up to rescue them as they have longed for me to do." (vs.5). Isaiah had multiple conversations with the Lord like the one we see recorded in Isaiah 6:8 as the Lord speaks, "Whom should I send as a messenger..?" and Isaiah answers, "Here I am, send me."

Jesus is my prime example (always). At His baptism, through the wilderness experience confronting Satan, and at Gethsemane to name a few, Jesus was in daily conversation with His Father. Some believers use this as an excuse when they do not hear the Lord speaking to them saying, "of course He heard the Father, that's Jesus". In other words, "Jesus is One of a kind and so of course would hear His Father". Yep, He is so special that he worked diligently to tell us that we could be like Him (please read John 17). In fact, that is a major reason He came to earth. Sorry folks but you cannot use that excuse because Jesus lives in us and has given us His full authority. Just sayin'.

In addition, at the end of this Holy book, we hear conversations between the Apostle John and Jesus as revelation pours fourth during his REST experiences before the Lord while in the Spirit. These proclamations, recorded by John, have significance in our future but also serves as a witness of encouragement to listen for the Lord. This last book of the bible ends with a conversation. Jesus says, "Yes I AM coming soon..." to which John answers, "Amen! Come Lord Jesus." (Revelations 22:21) Yep, another conversation.

I hope it is becoming clear that REST with the Lord God Almighty is not only needed but fulfills a desire of the Lord as well. I believe it is the one thing needed to stay grounded in The Truth for living our lives. Psalms 91, my favorite, begins with an instruction and ends with a promise. Listening to God, the Psalmist says, "Those who live in the shelter (secret place) of the Most High will find rest in the shadow of the Almighty."... (Ps 91:1)...He will cover you with His feathers. He will shelter you with His wings. His faithful promises are your armor and protection."(Ps 91:4) Now, please go read Psalms 91:11-16 which are Father God's promises to us if we will just REST in His shadow (which suggests we need to be close).

Appendix 2

How to REST

So, for me, REST stands for (Relaxed Engaged Simple Trusting). The bible shows different places to find REST. So let us look at a few.

As the first couple ever to be alive on earth walked in the 'cool of the day', they engaged their Creator. Further, in the Old Testament, we see it happening by a stream, in the tent of meeting, at the top of a mountain, from contemplative psalmists, and Moses in the wilderness. In the New Testament, we experience this dialogue on a mountaintop, in a garden, at a baptism and sitting at the feet of Jesus. Of course, there are multitudes of other examples of REST with the Lord.

For me folks, the best ones come from Jesus' life experiences. He even gives direction on how to set up a place for these sacred encounters as He taught in Matthew 6:6 saying, "But when you pray, go away by yourself, shut the door behind you and pray to your Father in private." I love the translation in the NASB as it finishes the verse saying, ":....and your Father who sees in secret will repay you." I just love Jesus' simplicity here, don't you?

So, let's get started. I have found that it is best if the journey begins with a desire to want a quiet time with your Savior. This is **KEY** folks. Desire determines devotion, devotion governs diligence, diligence fuels dedication and dedication yields victory. Here is the good news: only you can determine true desire. Don't' get me wrong, you can start with a simple willingness and discipline but if true desire isn't soon to be birthed, you may have to try again later. If that happens, it is not a failure rather simply a practice.

Another reason I have found this to be important is related to your #1 enemy (Satan). He is skilled with many effective devices that can help you be unsuccessful. One of his best strategies is distraction. If he can sidetrack you in the slightest, it will encourage him to continue until you quit your REST (which is his goal). He knows that distraction disengages which leads to destroy what 'good' your mind was set upon while in the quiet place behind the shut door. I have had many distractions in the 25 years I have been practicing this sacred REST. I have learned to act quickly as I sense its onset saying, "devil shut up, go back to hell or get permission from Jesus to mess with me. You only have two choices." "Now GO!!!!" You know what? He leaves because we are the ones with the authority from Jesus. Then I refocus on my picture of Jesus. Do not beat yourself up about losing a battle or two along the way. Even King David had problems as recorded in Psalms 22:2, "Every day I call on You, my God, but you do not answer." But in the very next verse, David proclaims, "Yet You are holy, enthroned on the praises of Israel." Even strong-willed Apostle Paul was recorded in Romans 6:19 as saying, "I want to do what is good but I don't. I don't want to do what is wrong but I do it anyway." But in a few verses later Paul proclaims, "Who will free from me this life that is dominated by sin and death? Thank God the answer is in Jesus Christ our Lord" (Romans 6:24-25).

So let us look at some steps as you begin this sacred journey of what I call "listening prayer". Begin by asking Father to strengthen your heart to be in agreement with His desire to enjoy quite time in the secret place with Him. Something like, "Lord I want a true desire. Please help my undesiring will to conform to Your heart's desire for me. I desire a loving engagement in Your shadow." (Go ahead do it NOW, I'll wait)…..Next, take some measured steps to prepare a place. Set a time for each day and pick a place where you can "shut the door" with no interruptions. Personally, I choose 5 am even though I was never an early riser. Yet I watched Jesus who also picked early morning. I do not think this time I have personally chosen is for everyone but for me, it is a moment when the day has yet to scream at me saying, "I need your attention here!". Rarely does anything or anyone invade my 5 am. Pick a place where you can be comfortable so that you can be comforted by your Unconditional Lover. I would recommend that you let others know that this is a sacred time and to please respect it. I have told Moms' with young children, "Maybe the only place for you in this season will be the bathroom". Yeah, I know!!

Once there in the quiet of the day, you have some options. You can choose a single focus of quiet time listening prayer. Alternatively, you may want to read scripture, a devotional book or other meaningful writings before entering this special time. Now ready for REST, start with a few cleansing breaths. Breathe in with your nose, hold it for a couple of seconds and <u>slowly</u> release the breath through your mouth. Be reminded that this is the way God gave the first Adam his very life. It can be very spiritual depending upon your focus at that moment. As your body relaxes, close your eyes and try to seek a picture of Jesus. For me, it is the Smiling Jesus or Laughing Jesus. I have found that it is helpful to picture Him in a physical place. I see Him at a huge tree, sitting in tall green soft grass near a flowing stream. Sometimes I can hear the water, or feel the breeze or even smell the grass. Usually, Jesus is sitting there with hands held open and His eyes expectantly on me. Please find your place.

Now is the time to speak silently or aloud words of praise or thanksgiving for Who He is to you. Paul tells us in 1 Thessalonians 5:16-18 that this IS the will of God. I would recommend not spending too much time here unless the Holy Spirit takes over and you cannot stop which would be great, right? Now is the time you quit talking or even thinking and just focus on Him. BE STILL and know He is there. [Shhhhhhhhhhhh] Hear your breathing, even the beat of your heart. Listen. Listen with an expectant heart. Be at peace in the presence of a loving God who is fully capable of sharing life with you. After all, He says in Jeremiah 29:12, "...you will call upon Me and I will listen to you" and in Jeremiah 29:13 "...you will seek Me and find Me when you search for Me with all your heart."

I would recommend starting with five minutes and extend it as your heart desires going forward. If you want, you can set a timer to remind you to end the time behind the shut door. But if you can, linger until you sense you two are through. Give Jesus a quick thank you for showing up before you leave. His desire is that we meet in that secret place often. Because the Lord is excited to be with you, He will always be there before you arrive. All it takes is a decision on your part followed by a dedication, driven by a desire.

Here are the steps:

+ Decide this is important to you

+ Select your room with the shut door

+ Get comfortable

+ Take a few cleansing breaths
  as you remember Adam coming to life as God "breathed on him"

+ Tell God Thanks and give Him praise

+ Close your eyes and find your picture of Jesus
  in His unique-to-you place

+ Shut up and listen up but do not tense up.
  Be confident that He is a truth teller and therefore He will speak to you even if you sense nothing in your soul (mind, will, emotions)

+ Close by thanking Jesus for His Faithfulness and for showing up

+ Leave refreshed by His Spirit

+ Repeat the above, tomorrow

DISCLAIMER: On most days, I do not sense His presence in my mind or soul. But then there are those early mornings that He is felt and that day makes up for all the others. The problem could be the way we read scripture. As we read, it can sound like a continual conversation with God and His creation and that He is even speaking audibly. The truth is that most of the time we are not told how He communicates. Is it just me, or do you have similar feelings when reading scripture? We simply do not always know how the biblical characters experienced these sacred encounters, do we? Personally, I do not believe that they were 'every day' conversations. Our heavenly Father 'speaks' how and when He wants. He is always on time and in His will.

Do not get discouraged when not 'sensing' His presence. That can play into another of your # 1 enemy's toolbox. To your #1 enemy, discouragement is delightful. Do not give the "father of all lies" this pleasure. Graham Cooke has a wonderful teaching on this topic of why we do not sense the Lord at times. His book is entitled, *Hiddenness & Manifestation*. I would highly recommend it as it is a quick read because it is powerful. It changed my perspective on the topic and gave me a peace going forward. You can find it a www.BrilliantBookhouse.com.

My thoughts:

Made in the USA
Lexington, KY
12 June 2019